Millionaire

How I Did It and You Can Too!

No part of this publication may be reproduced, stored in a retrieval system, or transmitted in any form or by any means, electronic, mechanical, photocopying, recording, scanning, translating, or otherwise, except as permitted by the United States' Copyright Act.

Limit of Liability/Disclaimer of Warranty: The author makes no representations or warranties with respect to the accuracy or completeness of the contents of this Book and specifically **disclaims any implied warranties of merchantability or fitness for a particular purpose**. No warranty may be created or extended by a sales representative or written sales material. The advice and strategies contained herein may not be suitable for your situation. You should consult with a professional where appropriate. The author shall have no liability for following this advice or strategy and shall have no liability for any loss profits or any commercial damages, including, but limited to, special, incidental, consequential, or other damages.

Copyright 2018 by J. Mitchell

Dedication: This Book is dedicated to anyone who wants to save at least one million dollars or more. This Book is not based on theory, concepts or a hypothesis. This Book is based on my actual, personal experience. It is not based on winning the lottery or some get rich quick scheme, although I have tried and failed (like many) at a few of those. No, this Book is how I have saved over a million dollars or more, and how, like me, you can do it too. By reading this short Book, you will gain all the tools and knowledge to become a millionaire. I really do believe that or else I would not have written this Book and wasted your time with you reading it. Won't you take the first step and buy this Book and read it? It is worth it.

Table of Contents

Preface — page 5

Chapter 1 – Introduction — page 7

Chapter 2 — page 11

Chapter 3 — page 17

Chapter 4 — page 25

Chapter 5 — page 31

Chapter 6 — page 38

Chapter 7 — page 43

Chapter 8 — page 55

Chapter 9 — page 64

Preface

Another financial book? There are a lot of financial books on the market and the advice given runs the gamut. I know because I have read over a hundred of these type books, and I have read numerous articles on personal finance. I read these books and articles because despite being a high school graduate and having three college degrees (two of which are on the graduate level), I was exposed to very little, if any, education on personal finance.

In high school and college, you are taught subjects such as History, Math, and English, but you are taught virtually nothing about money. You are not taught anything about managing and making financial decisions. At least, I was not. School does not cover reviewing a lease, opening a checking account, financing a car, obtaining a mortgage, taking on a credit card, or financing furniture. You are taught very little in school.

However, this Book is different than your schooling because it tells you how I became a millionaire. It tells you exactly what I did to save over a million dollars. But, the beauty is, you can do it too. This Book will tell you exactly how. It is not based on theory or a non-personal experience. It is based on my actual experience.

You've heard of, or maybe actually experienced, a stock broker calling his client and saying to his client you must purchase stock "XYZ." When the client asks the stock broker how much of "XYZ" does the stock broker own? The stock broker replies, "None." The stock broker is not bought into what he is selling. He does not believe enough in what he is selling to buy any of the stock himself.

In this case, I have bought into this advice. I have lived this. I have experienced this. I will tell you what has not worked for me. I will also tell you what has worked for me. I am not a genius. You do not need to be a genius to be a millionaire. I am also not deemed to be a "financial expert." And, you are probably not either. Notwithstanding that, however, by reading this Book and following my advice, you will learn how to succeed financially.

This Book is not long. It is intentionally short, so you will not get frustrated and not read it. But it is packed with useful advice that I used in reaching a million dollars saved. Please take the time to read it and follow the advice I provide. It may change your life.

Chapter 1 - Introduction

The main purpose of this Book is to teach you how I became a millionaire, so that you, likewise, can become one too. In school, you're taught a number of subjects, but you are not taught how to become a millionaire. You are not taught how to save money, invest or how to strike it rich. This Book will allow you to do just that because I did it myself. This is not a Book based on theories or scientific formulas. This is a Book where I will walk you step-by-step of how I saved over a million dollars. And, if I can do it, so can you. What I provide to you really works.

When I was going to Georgia Tech, during my Drown Proofing Class, I was taught that I would one day own a yacht. That I would be rich once I graduated. A job as an Engineer would provide me financial freedom, I was told. So, when I graduated from Georgia Tech and started my first job out of college for IBM, and that did not happen, I was disillusioned. I then tried everything.

One thing I tried, because quite frankly it sounded great, was multi-level marketing. The idea was that you would sell products offered by the multi-level marketing company to your friends. The profit would be the difference between what you paid for the products and what you sell the products for. The problem was that the products were not cheap. You were supposed to sell the "quality" of the products. Second, the multi-level marketing business was based on getting your friends to sell the products. If you signed up your friends to do this, you would make a fee off each product they sold. My experience was that I could sell some of the products, but I could not convince others to sign and sell the products as part of the multi-level marketing business. This then did not work for me in becoming a millionaire.

Another method I tried to strike it rich, and, to be truthful, still try at times, is the lottery. Georgia, like many States, has the Mega Millions and Powerball Lottery. I have bought lottery tickets, but I have never won more than ten dollars. Luckily, I only buy a few lottery tickets per year. But, for me, the lottery has not made me a millionaire.

I became an attorney in 1990. I had to go to Law School and pass the Georgia Bar, but doing that did not make me a millionaire. One method, I was told, to make a million dollars or more is to sign up a personal injury case. After graduating from Law School, I joined a small, personal injury law firm. While we settled cases over a million dollars, I never made much money in the law firm. I was paid a fairly low salary and received a few, small bonuses about every six to nine months. While attorneys (as well as those in other professions) do make a lot of money at one time, it did not occur or happen for me. Signing up large dollar personal injury cases is definitely a method to amass at least a million dollars; however, it did not work for me.

Another method I have tried to reach the million dollar mark was by participating, and hopefully winning, the Publisher's Clearing House Sweep Stakes ("PCH"). My experience with PCH was not a good one. I constantly received materials from PCH that requested me to subscribe to magazines or purchase products. I never did either. PCH stated it did not require the purchase of magazines or the purchase of any products, but PCH did require an entrant to continue to reply to its many requests to maintain your participation in the sweep stakes in order to become a winner. Needless to say, PCH did not work for me.

Many people think that a person can become a millionaire if you invent and patent a product. I came up with what I thought was a great idea. I manufactured and patented my product. I wrote letters to manufacturers of companies that should have been interested in my invention. Unfortunately, none of them were. This then was not a way for me to amass at least a million dollars. Admittedly, I thought I would make millions of dollars off my invention. I was truly excited, but only then to be ultimately disappointed. So, the invention and patent route to making a million dollars was a failure for me.

Investing in a new business venture is a means to accumulate at least a million dollars. Therefore, I heard from my neighbor about a wonderful business venture. It sounded like a great idea. The business venture involved investing in a virtual connoisseur ("VC") business. The business manufactured and produced VCs and placed such VCs in hotels, motels, restaurants, and numerous public locations. The VCs provided advertising and directions to businesses located near the VCs. The investor owned his or her VC, and the investor made money each month off advertising sales. To me, this sounded like a great business, and for several years, it was quite successful. Unfortunately, it ended up being a Ponzi Scheme. While I did not lose my investment money, I did not become a millionaire pursuing this endeavor.

If you try to get rich quick, based on my experience, you will fail. The people who are getting rich are those selling the get-rich-quick schemes. You should avoid these risky investments.

Well, at this point, you are probably wondering how did I become a millionaire? I will tell you in the following pages, but as you have read, I have tried many different avenues. And, maybe you have too. We have all made mistakes, but I have written this Book to let you know how it can be done. If I can do it, you can do it too, or at least, you can see how I did it and know that it can be done.

Let's go then! Let's start our journey. Just keep reading. It will not take you long to learn how I did it.

Point: Avoid Get Rich Quick Schemes. They will not work.

Chapter 2

The first step to reaching at least a million dollars is to live below your means. Simply put, this means spending less than you earn. You cannot save money and build your nest egg if you spend more money than you earn. For some people this means sticking to a strict budget. We did not stick to a strict budget, but it is not a bad idea.

To spend less then you make, you must review the income side of the equation and compare it to the spending side of the equation. If your income is not greater than your spending, then you have two options: (1) increase your income or (2) decrease your spending. Of course, you can do both.

You will need to determine your actual income and work to live below that level. You may have to cut your lifestyle. You may have to go without cable television, or you may have to subscribe to a cheaper cable television plan. You also may have to purchase and drive an older, used vehicle or use an off-brand cell phone. Be very careful about financing cars, furniture, a house, or other items over a period of years. The payments can hamper your ability to save money.

If you strap yourself to expensive purchases to live a better lifestyle, then you can prevent yourself from saving money. USA Today, the July 9, 2018 edition, reported that 1 in 5 workers said they do not save any of their annual income. You will not reach your one million dollars in saving goal if you do not save any of your income.

When you have a lot of payments and not much savings, then you get involved in get-rich-quick schemes, which, as I have stated, have never worked for me and do not work for a large majority of people. You need to be wary of these ventures. They will make you worse off, rather than better off.

Some people cannot spend less than they make. They then are in debt or are constantly trying to borrow money. This is not the way to accumulate at least a million dollars or more, and it is not the way you want to live your life.

In Charles Dickens' book <u>David Copperfield</u>, Mr. Micawber noted that if annual income is twenty pounds, but annual spending is 19.6, then happiness results. However, if annual income is twenty pounds, but annual expenditures are 20.6, then misery results. Charles Dickens' father could not live below his means and was therefore put into Debtors Prison for not adhering to this principle. The clear message or aim then is to spend less than what you make.

One way to spend less than what you make is to create a large income. I do not have a large income, but over the years, my income has increased on my job by getting promotions, receiving more responsibility, and obtaining cost of living increases to my income. I have also created income outside my full time job by: (1) teaching part time at a Law School, and (2) selling my textbook, via

Amazon, to the students who take my Class. I have also written Motions for attorneys and done some side legal work to increase my income. The point is you should try to increase your income by doing a good job in your current line of work and consider a side hustle. In other words, think of ways you can bring in additional income (ideally, without too much work or effort) by using the skills you currently have.

      The other side of the equation is to spend less money than you make. You have to pay your bills, but you can, and should, work to reduce your bills by: (1) negotiating lower car and homeowner's insurance rates each year or every other year (I have saved a lot of money by following this advice); (2) shop for a cheaper cell phone plan; (3) conserving energy by turning off your lights when you leave a room and using energy efficient light bulbs; (4) negotiating a lower cost with your heating/gas provider; and (5) negotiating a lower cost with your cable/television provider. One of your bills should be your personal retirement where you pay yourself at least once a month (more on this later in the Book). But the point is you can and should work to lower your spending, and at the same time, treat your retirement and savings as a bill you have to pay every month. If you go out to eat a lot consider going out less or going to a lower cost restaurant. The idea is to analyze your spending and work to reduce or cut your costs where you can.

      Two major ways to cut costs is to live in lower cost housing and drive economical vehicles. A good example of this is Warren Buffet who is one of the richest men in the world. He purchased his house in Omaha. Nebraska in 1955 for $31,500, and he still lives in it. My wife and I purchased the home we live in now for a reasonable price and still live in it thirty years later. While we have had to make repairs, and have made improvements, we have kept our overall expenses down because we have paid it off, and we do not live in a high property tax location. You should also look to purchase lower cost, economical vehicles. There is no need to drive the latest and greatest, snazzy vehicle. You need a vehicle that is dependable and will get you where you need to go. Both my wife and I have had great success driving Hondas, but you should pick out a car that is lower in cost and reliable.

The main point is if you minimize expenses, maximize income, and live simply, there is more of an opportunity to save, invest, and compound your savings. This will allow you to reach at least a million dollars in savings.

F. Scott Fitzgerald was famous for writing <u>The Great Gatsby</u>. Many a tenth grader has read this book. During his lifetime, F. Scott Fitzgerald made a lot of money off selling short stories and working in Hollywood. In 1929, a terrible year for the stock market, F. Scott Fitzgerald sold eight short stories to <u>The Saturday Evening Post</u> for $30,000. This was a large sum of money in 1929. His book royalties during his lifetime were not large, but he sold many short stories and made very good money off of those and his work in Hollywood.

The reason I am giving you this background is that throughout F. Scott Fitzgerald's lifetime, he was constantly spending more money than he made. In fact, he wrote a short story on this very topic. He had to borrow money often from his agent and publisher. He was a great writer, but he was terrible at managing his money. F. Scott Fitzgerald never purchased a home, although he had the means to do so. The few cars he purchased, he destroyed. He was constantly in debt. He spent more money than he made. This is not the recipe for amassing at least a million dollars. In a 1991 speech to Notre Dame, Warren Buffet said he had seen a lot of people fail "because of liquor and leverage." F. Scott Fitzgerald was an alcoholic and was a borrower of money from others.

In fact, F. Scott Fitzgerald wrote many stories, including <u>The Great Gatsby</u>, about the rich. He made judgments about those that were rich, and he realized money could buy a better education, a more luxurious lifestyle, and for him, more time to write novels. However, he could never manage his money. Fitzgerald was careless with his money, often spending it on booze, wild parties, and an overabundance of servants. The result was that money ruled his life, all because he had to earn money to squander it. Thus, in order to save the money, and reach your million dollar or more goal, you will have to find a way to handle, rather than squander, the money you earn.

There was a recent case in Atlanta where an attorney named Tex McIver, accused of killing his wife, was making over $500,000 per year. The jury ultimately found him guilty, but the surprising, revealing fact was despite being an attorney for many years, and a Partner in a large, well-known law firm, at age 75, he had nothing saved. He spent $25,000 a month on a farm, and his expenses were more than his income. The State of Georgia presented this testimony as a motive for murdering his wife.

The key point to remember is that you cannot save more than a million dollars if you spend more than you make.

Point: You must spend less than you make. In other words, you must live below your means.

Chapter 3

Once you figure out how to spend less than you make, you need to pay off your debt(s) (except, for now, your mortgage). Through my life, like many people, I have incurred car loans, credit card debt, a mortgage on a condo, and a home mortgage. Of course, like many people, I have incurred more than one of the foregoing list of debts. Many people also have student loan debt; I have paid for my son's private school, my son's college, my wife's college, and my post college degrees. I have done this by saving money using a savings account and a 529 Plan and via cash flow. Thus, I have not incurred college or school debt, but I have incurred a lot of debt, otherwise.

Debt is definitely a problem for most Americans. Dave Ramsey's book, <u>Financial Peace</u>, reports that the average credit card holder carriers a balance of over $8,000 per month, paying an average of 18.3 percent in interest. <u>Money</u> magazine's June/July 2018 issue reports that Americans' debt hit a new high of $13 trillion dollars last year and that amount surpasses the previous record set in 2008 by $280 billion. People get stressed out over debt, no matter how high or low your income level. Yet, people still charge or pile on the debt not realizing the full impact on savings. <u>Consumer Reports</u> found that the typical household has $38,000 in debt. Further, it has been reported that seventy percent of people do not pay off their credit card balance every month. Research has shown that financial strain caused by debt lowers people's sense of well-being.

I have not had credit card debt like most Americans. With credit cards, we have paid off the debt incurred at each month's end. But if you cannot do this and are currently using credit cards, you need get on a plan and pay off the balances. Dave Ramsey outlines a method to deal with credit card debt; he states: (1) you should stop using credit cards by cutting them up, and (2) pay off the credit card balances. He says that you pay off the balances by: (1) listing the credit card balances from lowest balance to highest balance; (2) making the minimum payments on all credit cards, except your lowest balance; (3) you then pay the minimum payment on the lowest balanced credit card plus make payment toward the principal; you do this by attacking the lowest balanced credit card until it is paid off; and (4) once it is paid off, you attack the next lowest balance credit card until all credit cards are paid off. I personally, as stated, unlike suggested by Dave Ramsey, use credit cards, but as stated, we pay the balances off each month. We've been able to succeed doing that, but you will need to decide what works best for you and your family. If you are carrying credit card balances from month-to-month, you need to stop using credit cards if you want to be financially successful.

A credit counseling survey found that seventy-one percent of Americans say debts are making their lives unhappy. Money magazine's June/July 2018 issue reports that people's peak earning years also are their peak debt years. The study found that people between the ages of 45 and 54 reported the highest levels of debt overall, totaling $134,600, and those in the 35 to 44 age range carried the second largest amount at $133,100. There have also been studies that have found that money does significantly contribute to contentment. But with debt, there are psychological costs and burdens of worry and life dissatisfaction. Therefore, you need to work hard to pay off your debt, and work to not incur additional debt, as fast as possible. This will enable you to reach the million dollars mark in savings.

Cars can be expensive. If you finance a car at 5% or 7%, then not paying the finance charge over a number of years would be helpful in your quest. You save money by not financing your car purchase. However, not everyone can afford to pay cash for a new car, so you should look to purchase a used car. My wife and I have purchased used cars, and this has saved us money by avoiding finance charges.

Of course, you would rather purchase a new car, but you can save thousands of dollars, avoid finance charges, and reach your saving's goal (of at least a million dollars) if you, instead, purchase a used car. If you do this, you will also save money on car insurance. The rates will typically be cheaper on a used car as opposed to a new car.

If you purchase a used car, it would be wise to purchase a reliable, less costly, good on gas mileage vehicle. If you can save on the purchase price, and also have a used car that breaks down less, that will help you reach your goal of saving money and in reaching the million dollar mark. You want a car that does not drink a lot of gas. My wife and I, as mentioned earlier, purchased Hondas, both used and new, and we have had good success, but you will have to make your own decisions. These are some pointers, however, that have helped us.

You should avoid leasing a car. When you lease, you lease a new car, based on my experience. A new car carries with it higher insurance costs. Also, when you lease, the interest or finance rate is not revealed to you, so that means your finance charge could be very high. You also are limited in the number of miles you can put on the car. If you exceed the number of miles per year, then you will have to pay a mileage fee, which can be quite expensive.

It is reported that leasing a car is the most expensive method to operate a car. The benefit of leasing is you can drive a new car every three to five years by making the lease payments. You also may be able to deduct the costs of leasing if used in your business. The detriment is: (1) you usually have to make a down payment; (2) you are limited to the number of miles you can drive per year and any overage is subject to a mileage charge; and (3) at the end of the lease, you have nothing to show for all your payments. Based on my experience of leasing cars, I would avoid leasing.

When purchasing a new or used car make sure you haggle with the price or financing terms or warranty, etc. You can shop online with multiple dealers in and around your area and do the haggling online to ensure you get the best deal. Then, when at the dealer, you can haggle more.

If need be, do like I did, and ask them to also give you a few free t-shirts after you have agreed to the price. The point is make sure you haggle to try to obtain your best deal and this will help you reach your savings goal.

      Auto loans, based on my experience, can be rotten. During my life, my wife and I have taken out car loans to purchase our vehicles. Where we got into trouble was rolling the debt of a prior car into the new purchase. Because the value of the car goes down faster than the loan balance, we found ourselves increasing the balance owed on a depreciating asset. I have read that the typical auto loan today is for $375 per month over a fifty-five month period. That amount is a lot to pay per month and is too long a period to finance a car. The reason why is the value of the car drops faster than the loan balance. That was definitely what we experienced. What we finally had to do was buckle down, and as we made our monthly payments, we paid extra toward the principal. Eventually, we were able to pay off the loans. Now, we save money, on a monthly basis, as part of our emergency fund (more on this in the next Chapter), and pay cash for our car purchases.

      The key point of this Chapter is you must work hard to pay off your debts. If you pay off your credit card debt, that is the simplest and easiest way to earn 18% on your money. Not having to pay those high rate credit cards is as good as earning 18% on your money. Plus, it is both a tax-free and a risk-free investment. Try to pay off your credit cards as soon as possible This will be a great step toward your million dollars saved goal.

You should also work hard to pay off your auto loans, payday loans (if applicable), and any pawn shop loans. You will need to work to pay off these debts as fast as possible. As stated, and is worth mentioning again, the best way to do this is to make minimum payments on each debt and pay off the smallest to largest debts, in that order. You pay off the smallest debt first and then attack each debt one at a time until all debt is paid off.

Based on my personal experience, it is a wonderful feeling when you pay off your debts. Not having credit card debt, an auto loan, student loan, or a mortgage hanging over your head gives you great peace of mind. It makes it easier to sleep at night. It also allows you to save money and gain traction on your million dollars in savings goal. Instead of paying money to a creditor, you save it.

Dave Ramsey, on his radio show, likes to quote a Bible verse that is in Proverbs. It is from Proverbs 22:7 and it states that "Rich rule over the poor and the borrower is a slave to the lender." When you are in debt, you do feel like you are working for your creditor(s), but when you have paid off the debt(s), there is a freedom that you do feel. You no longer feel like you are serving the entity that lent you the money.

A few final comments about debt. First, beware of the cash advance. If you get a cash advance on your credit card, the minute you receive the cash advance, you begin paying interest in the payment made with the check. Plus, all the other associated charges accrue, even if you are the type that pays off his or her credit card charges during the allotted grace period. Second, avoid borrowing from pawnshops. In some states, pawnshops charge annual interest rates of 200% or more. Finally, be careful taking out student loans for your son or daughter. The number of older Americans taking on student debt on behalf of their children and grandchildren has quadrupled in the past decade, with consumers over 60 now (this was reported in 2017) holding $66.7 billion in student loan debt. This is according to a report by the Consumer Protection Bureau. The skyrocketing costs of college has placed a burden on older Americans who take out loans for their child.

If you must borrow, here is a list of tips: (1) borrow on a short time period (for example, if it is a mortgage, take out a 15 year mortgage instead of a 30 year mortgage; or if it is a car loan, borrow on 3 years instead of 5 years); (2) borrow on items that go up in value if at all possible (for example, do not borrow money to go on a vacation); (3) buy less or a lower cost home or car or what you are purchasing, so you can pay it off faster; (4) make sure you borrow at a low interest rate; and (5) as mentioned above in the example, and is worth mentioning again in this list of tips, try to finance your home purchase on a 15 year, instead of a 30 year, mortgage or home loan (for a small difference in payment, you can save a huge amount of money over the life of the loan).

The last point in this Chapter to remember is that most borrowing is an anti-investment. It generates negative returns. In other words, if you can delay instant gratification, it will help you save money. Paying off debt will greatly improve your finances (it worked for me). It will allow you to reach the million dollars mark.

> **Point:** You must get out of debt. To get out of debt, pay off your debts as soon as possible, and quit borrowing money.

Chapter 4

There are three basic reasons for saving money. One reason is to save up to buy an item or put a down payment on a purchase. Another reason for saving is to build wealth (that, by the way, is what we will discuss in more detail later in this Book). Yet a third reason is to create an emergency fund. An emergency fund is there to help you when you have an unexpected expense.

An emergency fund is present for any expenses that arise in the event of a true emergency. If you lose your job, then you have an emergency fund to pay for your expenses until you get another job. You should build up three to six months of expenses in your emergency fund.

The reason for an emergency fund is that if you are like most people, something that you own is going to break. Just within the last six months, my car broke down and so did our refrigerator. With respect to my car, I needed to replace my starter, and that cost, including getting my car towed, over $600. Replacing my refrigerator cost me $585 (which is a relatively low cost for refrigerators). And, at the end of last year, my upstairs heater needed replacing and that cost us $1,800. I have also had to replace my downstairs air conditioner, and my hot water heater in the last couple of years. The point of this is that you need money in case of an emergency. You therefore must create an emergency fund.

To build security, you need a way to deal with unexpected expenses. You should start small with building your emergency fund. Initially, do not worry about having a large amount of money in your emergency fund. $500 to $1,000 is enough to cover many unwelcome expenses, such as a car repair or a medical bill.

I have an emergency fund and place those funds in a money market account in a different bank than where I regularly bank. In other words, my savings and checking account are in a different bank than my emergency fund. In this way, I can separate the emergency fund from the regular, daily needs type fund. If you spend the emergency fund on a car repair, for instance, you will then need to replenish the emergency fund, so you will be ready when the next emergency comes (not in the event the next emergency comes, because it will).

An unexpected cost will occur in your life. You do not know when it will happen, but it will happen. If you drive a car, eventually, it will need a repair. If you, or a loved one, gets sick, there will be a need to go to the doctor and this will incur a medical bill. Also, people lose their jobs. The point is you have to have a plan in place for these type of events.

I plan, and I am advising you likewise to plan, by setting up an emergency fund. As stated, start your emergency fund small to begin with, but after you have paid off your debt(s) (except your mortgage), you should focus on boosting your emergency fund from $500 to $1,000 in savings to three to six months of required expenses. You should not be concerned with the interest rate or rate of return on your emergency fund. You are using this money in case of an emergency only. Placing this money in a bank savings account or money market account is acceptable.

Saving a few hundred dollars in an emergency fund can help reduce short-term, high-cost borrowing. In a recent Harris Poll (May 2018) almost two thirds of homeowners say they experienced home repair costs that caused them a lot of anxiety. Emergency funds, remember, are meant to be spent on emergencies. I read where a financial expert did a study and found that many people with an emergency fund are reluctant to part with this money even in the case of an emergency, but you should remember that is what the money in the emergency fund is there for. On the other hand, many people give up on creating an emergency fund because it gets quickly wiped out by unexpected expenses. However, that is exactly why you should create an emergency fund. Those funds can keep expenses being incurred on a credit card or borrowing from pay day lenders.

If the emergency fund needs to be used, then use the money in the fund, and then add back to it over time. In other words, there will be both additions and subtractions as life unfolds. Here are a few points to consider about an emergency fund: (1) set up a dedicated account; (2) automate (if you can) saving a preset amount per month into an emergency fund; (3) if you cannot automate it, then make a rule to set aside a specific amount per month into your dedicated emergency fund; and (4) do not stop putting money into it until you build it up to at least three months' worth of expenses. It is important if you fall below this level to ensure you keep placing money into this account in your emergency fund, and do not be afraid to use it in case of an emergency. That is what it is there for.

I place my emergency fund in a money market account in a different bank than where I typically bank. I do this to place an emphasis on the fact that this is where my emergency money is located. I put money in this account one time a month. As I remove this money to spend on items such as repairs, the replacement of broken items, cars, or vacations (I realize vacations are not emergencies, but I use my emergency account for vacations, at times), I replenish the funds over a period of months. My point here is for you to: (1) get in the habit of placing money in an emergency fund, and (2) when you access such funds for an emergency, you need to work to replenish the funds as soon as you can.

How does this help you reach at least one million dollars in savings, you may be wondering? Well, if you do not have the cash to pay for an emergency (say, my recent car repair for $600), then you will have to borrow the money. If you borrow the money on a credit card at 18% interest, then this can work against your goal of saving money to reach at least one million dollars. You do not want to be paying on a credit card for years on a repair of $600 for your car.

In an article in the Atlanta Journal and Constitution, dated March 11, 2018, it stated that 26% of those age 75 and older still had credit card debt. The article found that this is a 159% increase since 1989. Make sure then you have an emergency fund to pay for these costs, so you will not be in the same situation.

You want to make sure that you can easily access the money. You do not want to invest the money in unliquidated assets or an asset that is not easily converted to cash quickly. You do not want your emergency money invested in a bank or investment company that will not send you the funds quickly, in other words. You need immediate access to the money. So, you should keep the funds in a simple savings or checking or money market account at a bank or credit union. Do not worry about your return on your emergency fund dollars.

While you need to have an emergency fund and ensure the funds are readily available, you also need them separate from your regular savings or checking account. In other words, the emergency fund is not there to pay your monthly bills (unless, of course, you lose your job). Therefore, place your emergency fund in a different account than your regular savings or checking account. As mentioned, I do this by placing my emergency account in a different bank altogether than my regular savings and checking account.

A fully funded emergency fund will have $10,000 to $15,000 in the account. When you have this amount in the emergency fund, you will be tempted to invest it in the stock market or mutual funds or ETFs or real estate or some other investment to attempt to maximize your investment. You need to resist this temptation. The money is there not to earn a great return, but, instead to be there when an emergency comes, and it will hit. So, it is fine to have the emergency fund in a money market account or regular checking or savings account. It is an emergency fund, not an investment fund. It is much like insurance; it is there to protect you when you have an emergency.

Based on personal experience, it is great having an emergency fund in place. The reason I say that is when my car starter needed to be replaced (along with the towing charge), and my upstairs heating unit broke down, it was a great relief to have the money available to pay these unexpected, non-budgeted costs.

Point: You must have an emergency fund. You will have an unexpected expense in your life, and you will need to use funds in the emergency fund to deal with such expenses. You do not want to have credit card debt.

Chapter 5

The best way to build wealth, and do it quicker, is to do so tax free. Of course, you want to do it legally. It just makes sense to build savings up without paying taxes, doesn't it? If you can save money, without paying taxes on it, legally, while in the savings account, you will build up the account faster than if you had to pay taxes on it. The way to do that is to take advantage of a 401(k) or 403 (b) and/or an IRA or Roth IRA.

A 401(k) is a saving plan that will help fund your retirement. If you work for a nonprofit organization, then a similar plan is known as a 403 (b) plan, or if you work for a local or state government, then it is called a 457 plan (for purposes of this discussion, I am going to use the term "401(k)" because that is what I have available at my employer). These numbers (401(k), 403 (b) and 457) line up with the applicable section in the Internal Revenue Code.

The way they work is you contribute a specified portion (typically a percentage) of your salary to the plan. You can and should have it automatically deducted from your paycheck. You pick a savings vehicle (ie – a 2030 target retirement mutual fund in Vanguard). The amount contributed (unless it is a Roth 401(k)) is excluded from your taxes, and the earnings accumulate tax free until you withdraw the money. Because you are not paying taxes on the dividends or capital gains, the money can grow faster. There is a limit (based again on the IRS code sections) you can contribute per year.

One of the best features of these plans (other than tax free contributions and accumulations) is that with many, your employer will also make a matching contribution into the plan. A typical employer contribution is 50% of the amount you contribute up to a specified percentage of your compensation. Usually, capped at 6% of your salary. As an example: say you make $30,000 per year and have a plan allowing you to contribute 10% of your salary to a 401(k) retirement plan. Then, you could contribute $3,000 per year to the 401(k) retirement plan. 6% of your salary is $1,800 (6% * $30k), which is the maximum your employer will match, but your employer will contribute 50% of that maximum, so it is $900. The employer match, however, is free money paid to you in your 401(k) retirement plan, and it grows tax free. If your employer matches your contribution, then you should earn the maximum match by maxing out the amount you invest in the plan.

The standard 401(k) plan has limited options you can invest in, mainly mutual funds. You should choose one based on your goals, but the best approach is to pick an index fund that is geared toward your projected retirement date (ie – a 2030 target date mutual fund in Vanguard, if available). Make sure you are investing in your future year in and year out. Make sure you take full advantage of your company's match that you are offered at work through your company's 401(k) (or similar retirement plan). Do so even if you are paying off deft, because a company match is free money. Even if you cannot contribute enough to meet your retirement goal right now, start contributing immediately and increase the amount over time.

Less than one-third of Americans are saving in their 401(k)s or other workplace retirement accounts, according to an analysis of tax records by the Census Bureau researchers. The research was done on W-2 tax forms from 2012 to 2015 from 155 million workers. It found that nearly 80 % of Americans work for an employer that offers a retirement program such as a 401(k), 403b, etc., but only 32% of workers sign up for such accounts. This is a problem because the most conservative calculations estimate that Americans will need to have about 8 to 10 times their annual salary saved for retirement.

The net–net: you need to join a retirement plan and save at least something as soon as possible.

An IRA or a Roth IRA is also a way to save. The money inside the IRA or Roth IRA accumulates tax free. Like the 401(k) or 403 (b) there are limits on the amount you can contribute per year and with a Roth IRA there is an annual income limit that limits your usage of the Roth IRA, but you should try to take advantage of either the IRA or Roth IRA.

A think a simple way to save for retirement is to employ the 401(k) of your employer and automatically join it and contribute to it, at least to the amount of the company match. However, as mentioned, another way to save simply is to use the individual retirement account called an IRA or the Roth IRA. I have used both the IRA and the Roth IRA depending on my circumstances. I use Vanguard to handle my Roth IRA. If you earn a pay check, you can invest in a mutual fund (ie – a 2030 target date fund with Vanguard) using an IRA or a Roth IRA. Currently, you are limited to $ 5,500 per year (or $ 6,500 if age 50 or over). I would recommend investing in a Roth IRA, if you qualify (you can ask Vanguard for the income limits) or an IRA if you do not qualify. The dividends, interest and growth of the fund, within the IRA or Roth IRA, grow tax free. Basically, the IRS will not require you pay taxes on this investment while it is held within the IRA or Roth IRA. If an IRA, you will have to pay tax when you withdraw the money, but if it is a Roth IRA, you will not have to pay taxes on the withdrawals unless you withdraw the money prior to age 59 ½ (with exceptions).

As an example, if you save $5,000 per year, over a 45 year period, at 8% interest per year, the final accumulated amount is over $2,000,000. Using this method of saving, you are able to easily reach your goal of over a million dollars saved, especially, since the income produced within an IRA or Roth IRA accumulates tax free.

If you open and use a Roth IRA, the money you place in the Roth IRA is not deductible from your taxes (so you pay tax on the amount), but the earnings accumulate tax free. The great benefit about the Roth IRA is, while there is no upfront tax benefit, there are no taxes to pay when you withdraw the funds, like with an IRA.

There are disadvantages of these tax-advantaged retirement plans. With a few exceptions, you cannot withdraw the funds from the retirement plan until you reach the age of 59 ½ without a 10% penalty, and paying the applicable income taxes. Also, if you withdraw the funds, you will not receive the benefit of tax-free earnings within the plan(s). However, keeping the money within the retirement plan(s) is really to your benefit if you want to reach the million dollars in savings figure.

Whether your employer contributes to your 401 (k) or not, you should still contribute and save money in it. Why? Because: (1) the money within the plan increases or grows tax free until you withdraw it; (2) it is an easier way to save money to reach your goal; and (3) the contributions to the plan are tax free, so you avoid paying tax on the money, at least initially and while in the plan.

When investing your money in a 401(k) invest in what does best over the long-term which is stock mutual funds or index funds. You do not want to invest in money market funds or Certificate of Deposits (CDs). I invest in three different type of funds: (1) a target retirement fund; (2) a balanced fund; and (3) a blue-chip growth fund. But you will need to decide yourself what you want to invest in. If you invest money on a consistent basis in these type funds I employ, however, you will reach your goal of saving at least one million dollars. You do not want to switch in and out of the market. Studies have shown market timing does not work.

In your 401(k), you do not want to invest too conservatively. Even if you are approaching retirement you do not want to invest all your funds in money market funds or CDs. Maybe some of it can be moved into those more conservative funds as you near retirement, but you could live another twenty or thirty more years after you retire, so you will need to retain about fifty percent still in stock mutual funds.

You also do not want to invest your 401(k) money in company stock. Maybe you put no more than ten percent in your company stock in your 401(k), but do not invest any more money into your company's stock in your 401(k). I do not purchase any company stock in my 401(k). Enron is a good example where employees lost their job, and their 401(k) retirement savings for those who held Enron stock in their 401(k) when Enron went bankrupt. You already have your job riding on your employer's health, so do not also have your 401(k) retirement savings riding on your employer's health too.

Personally, I use Vanguard. My employer uses Vanguard, and I contribute to my 401(k). To save at least a million dollars, you should make sure you join your company's 401(k) or similar plan and contribute to it. Pick a fund or funds that are target or balance funds and increase the percentage contributed per year to reach the maximum you can contribute to the plan. Make sure you get, at least, the company match. Remember, it is free money. This tax-free savings plan will increase over time.

Also, insure that your dividends (or the money that the account is producing) is automatically reinvested. In this way, your money will be making money off the money it produces. Additionally, you should insure that the money placed in your 401 (k) is automatically deducted from your pay check. In this way, you are forced to save. Again, the savings accumulate tax free until such funds are withdrawn.

Does this work? In other words, can you accumulate at least a million dollars in a 401(k) plan and/or an IRA/Roth IRA? The answer is yes. A lot of financial books you read will tell you to follow these steps, but the author of these financial books does not say whether or not he or she has personally followed this advice, and if it has worked for him or her. I can tell you that it has worked for me, and it will work for you (I truly believe), if you follow this advice.

Point: The best way to accumulate wealth (I have found) is to contribute to a retirement plan such as a 401(k), IRA or Roth IRA. You should join your company's retirement plan and contribute to the plan automatically. Pick a target retirement fund to make it easy. Increase your contributions over the year(s) until you hit the maximum allowed by the IRS code.

Chapter 6

One of the best ways to build wealth and get to your one million dollars in savings amount is to purchase a house or condo. Early in my career, my wife and I purchased a home, and because we moved, due to my job, we bought and sold a few homes and a townhouse. But the advantage of purchasing and owning a home is that it provides a place to live, and it allows you to build equity as you make payments toward the principal.

In our current home, we initially financed our house over a thirty (30) year period. We procured a fixed-rate, conventional loan. We later refinanced the thirty (30) year mortgage into a fixed rate conventional mortgage payable over a fifteen (15) year period. Eventually, through paying down debt, we were able to pay more toward the principal on this loan and pay off our mortgage. I did this prior to turning forty years old, so it can be done.

One note regarding a fixed interest rate, conventional mortgage: if you take out a loan on your home or condo without putting at least 20% down on the purchase price of the home or condo, then the mortgage lender will charge you private mortgage insurance or PMI. PMI is there to protect the lender or bank in case you default on the mortgage. Once you pay the loan down to 80% as a percentage of the loan to the value of your home, then you can request the lender or bank to drop PMI coverage. Your lender or bank may not be willing to do this, but you should ask what your lender or bank needs to drop PMI. Then, once you find that out, then follow their requests. Usually, a new survey will be required. But it will save you money if you can drop PMI from your monthly payment. The PMI, by the way, is not for your benefit; it is for the lender or bank's benefit. It is present to protect the lender or bank.

Early in my career, when we purchased our first home, we took out an adjustable rate loan. That was a mistake. The rate adjusted higher, and it made our monthly payments increase. Do not let your realtor talk you into taking out an adjustable rate mortgage. It is a big mistake. Also, do not take out a balloon loan (one that requires all the money be paid back after 5 years). We never did take out a balloon mortgage or loan, but I have heard others who did that and later regretted it.

In fact, it has been reported that the worse home loans are adjustable rate mortgages or ARMS. These mortgages adjust, usually, annually based on what another rate (ie – LIBOR) does. Most of these adjustable rate loans are based on an index. A fixed rate, shorter term loan on your home is your better choice. Ideally, of course, it would be great to pay cash for your home or condo, but few people can do that. We could not. In 1929 only 2% of American homes had mortgages on them; forty years later only 2% of American homes did not have mortgages on them. So, more likely than not, you will need to take out a mortgage to purchase your home or condo.

The adjustable rate mortgage, as I recall, came out in the 1980s. As mentioned, we took one out, and I would definitely avoid this type mortgage. They were there to allow a home owner to buy a home or condo at a lower interest rate, but the interest rate would adjust upward (We never had the rate adjust lower, and I have never heard of it adjusting down). From a lender or bank's stand point, the ARM is great because the lender or bank is protected from having lent money at a low interest rate when rates are later increased. The ARM is designed to protect the lender or bank when rates are rising from getting stuck with a lot of low interest loans. In other words, an ARM is designed to protect the lender or bank, not you. My realtor never explained this to me and my wife, and I, like many people, did not know it at the time. My realtor, in my opinion, just wanted to make a sale. The ARM, as you can see, transfers the risk of rates rising to you, the buyer, not to the lender or bank. You should avoid the ARM and just take out a fixed interest rate, conventional loan.

As I write this short Book, interest rates are low, so it makes sense to fix your interest rate. If you are in an ARM now, I would recommend you look to refinance as soon as possible prior to your interest rate adjustment.

The experts have differing advice on the percentage of your gross income you should borrow to purchase a house. Some people say no more than 35% and others 25%. Needless to say, you do not want to borrow so much that you cannot pay your bills, pay off all your debts (if you still have any by the time you purchase your home or condo), have an emergency fund and invest for retirement.

My advice is to try to stay close to 20% of your gross income to pay on your mortgage. As stated, some people say higher, but it is best to limit the payment to not more than 20% of your gross income. Also, you should avoid adjustable rate mortgages and balloon loans (as previously stated). You should try your best to take out a conventional, fixed rate loan on a fifteen (or less) year mortgage. As an example, of the 20% rule, if your gross income is $100,000 per year, then 20% is $20,000; divide that by 12 months and your principal and interest should be $1,666 per month.

Once you pay off your mortgage, you should take the payment you were making on the mortgage and invest those funds (more on that in a later Chapter). I did not do this initially, and that was a big mistake for me. Do not make the same mistake I initially made. You should just simply use the payment you were making on your mortgage (which is now paid off) and place that money in an investment in your retirement fund.

My wife and I also purchased a condo. We took out a thirty (30) year, fixed rate, conventional mortgage to do so, despite my advice above. As I said, if you can, it is much better to take out a fifteen (15) year, fixed rate, conventional mortgage. What we did, however, is (after creating an emergency fund, paying off all debt except for this mortgage and joining my company's 401(k) plan) made payments toward the loan's principal. When you do this, you should ensure that the additional payment(s) is designated to be applied to principal. I messed up once in my extra payment and a portion of that payment was applied to interest.

I encourage you to purchase a house or condo, when the time comes in your process as I have described in this little Book, which will help you to reach your million dollars saved goal. Building equity in a home or condo and eventually having no mortgage is a great feeling, and I know you can reach that target.

> **Point:** A great way to accumulate wealth is to purchase a house or condo. Do this after you have paid off debt, created an emergency fund and joined your company's 401(k) plan. Take out a fixed rate, conventional mortgage to purchase the home or condo. Limit the loan to no greater than 20% of your gross income and try to take out a 15 year mortgage, instead of a 30 year mortgage.

Chapter 7

If you have paid off your debt, created an emergency fund and started saving in your 401(k) retirement plan (or similar plan), then the best way I have found to build wealth and amass over a million dollars is to save and invest your money on a regular basis. To do this, I created a simple one page savings sheet where I listed the amount I wanted to save and invest and the date when I wanted to save the money and invest it. I also have an open space to write in what investment I placed my money. I had the amount I wanted to save listed on an every other week basis. I then started to invest every other week.

You can make your first investment into an IRA or Roth IRA (if you qualify). Once you hit the maximum number you can save per year, then you start investing outside your retirement plans. You need to do this on a regular, consistent basis just like you pay your bills. You should not skip this payment, just like you would not go without paying your water bill. And, think about this, isn't paying your retirement bill, or building _**your**_ wealth, more important than paying your cable or television bill?

An Atlanta Journal and Constitution article (dated April 29, 2018) reported that GoBankingRates.com found that 42% of Americans have less than $10,000 saved for retirement. The survey also found about 14% of the participants said they had saved absolutely nothing. You cannot be in this situation. You must save money and plan for your retirement.

I invest in two different places. I invest with Vanguard and also, with Scottrade, now Ameritrade. But you can use other, low cost providers. I picked these two because they are two of the lowest cost choices. With Vanguard, it has some of the lowest expense mutual funds and exchange-traded-funds ("ETFs"). In <u>The Elements of Investing</u>, by Charles D. Ellis, he says the best approach to investing is to keep investing expenses to a minimum. Warren Buffet says, "Performance comes, performance goes. Fees never falter." So, keep your investment fees low.

You need to plan and set up your personal or family expenses or bills such that you are able to save some amount of money each month. Remember this: ***Some savings is better than no savings, even if it is just a small amount***. If you can make the savings automatic that would be great. That way it is taken right out of your paycheck without having to worry about writing a check or moving money from your bank account to the savings investments. In other words, if you can set it up so that your employer takes a set percentage or amount from your paycheck, and it is placed into a 401 (k) or IRA that would be ideal. I currently do that, and it has worked great for me, and I am sure it will also work great for you too in helping you reach your savings goal. The point is you need to set up your finances, so that you are saving some amount per month so that you will feel more financially secure. Your standard of living will also improve if you are saving money, and you will be well on your way to reaching your one million dollars in savings objective.

Think about this: getting a high rate of return or interest rate on your savings or investments does not mean anything if you cannot save money in the first place. Having money deducted from your paycheck into a 401(k) or IRA is the best way, I have found, to force you to save if you are having any trouble saving. This will make you save.

To build your million dollars (or more) in savings, you must save money. You must save money out of every pay check you receive. If you do not save and make an intentional effort to save money out of every pay check you receive, you will not reach your goal. You should have a goal of saving a set amount from every pay check. If possible, do this automatically, so that percentage is taken out of each pay check and ideally placed into a retirement account, such as a 401(k). You work very hard at your job to bring home a pay check. You do not want your pay check to be a clearing house for people you owe money and for the items you purchase only. You do not want your money to come in to your account, and then all your money be paid to third parties (ie – the power company, gas company, water company, etc.) without you saving anything, even if, to begin with, a small percentage. You must get in the habit of saving money. Make absolutely sure that "YOU" are listed in your list of bills to pay and that you are paid too. You should be paid first.

The best way to save money, I have found, is to save a percentage or set amount from each pay check (or each time you are paid). It is very hard to save a large amount at one time. In other words, you place money in your 401(k) and/or Roth IRA and/or savings account (or ETFS/mutual funds) on a regular, consistent basis; you invest a small amount at a time. You want to save money in small steps, little by little. As you do this, you will see it grow. Based on my experience, it is much harder to save a large amount at one time, than to save a little at a time on a consistent basis.

In the next Chapter, I will discuss some of the mutual funds, stocks and ETFs I invest in or what to focus on and why. But before you decide in what to invest in, you must remember to place an importance on saving and investing to build your financial security.

As stated at the beginning of this Chapter, the way I have accumulated wealth is to save and invest money on a regular, consistent basis. Make it just like you are paying your bills. Save on a consistent and regular basis. Maybe for you it is once a month. For me, it is saving and investing twice a month. I save a set amount in different stocks or mutual funds or ETFs and do that on a consistent basis.

You will find from authorities in the Finance field that the best way to reduce your emotions when you invest is to invest on a regular basis. The experts on this process call it "dollar-cost averaging." When the market is down, you buy low. When the market is high, you are buying at a higher price. Warren Buffet, the great investor, is quoted on this idea saying, "Do not think of yourself as merely owning a piece of paper whose price wiggles around daily and that is a candidate for sale when some economic or political event makes you nervous. Instead, visualize yourself as a part-time owner of a business that you expect to stay with indefinitely, much as you might if you owned a farm or apartment house partnership with members of your family."

If you don't trust me, or the experts on this concept, then trust the Bible. In Proverbs 13: 11, it states, "Dishonest money dwindles away, **but he who gathers money little by little makes it grow.**"

You also should not try to time the market. Numerous studies have found that market timing just does not work. Peter Lynch, another great investor, said that all major advances and declines in the stock market have come as surprises to him. Therefore, if such market swings are surprises to him, then they would be for you and me too. Advice from many of the Financial experts is to not try to predict the stock market but to invest in the S&P 500 index or buy great companies at undervalued or underappreciated prices on a regular cadence.

Compounding, or compounding interest, is the concept of earning interest on interest; in other words, having your saved money make money. It is a way to supersize your savings and investments. Albert Einstein called compounding "the most powerful force in the universe." You do not have to be a genius to take advantage of it; you should get into the habit of saving an amount from each paycheck. Your money will start making money for you right away, increasing the chances you will meet your financial goal of at least a million dollars saved. The point here is to start saving as soon as you can. Make it a priority to save some amount from each paycheck you receive.

A formula to calculate how much your money will compound or grow over a number of years is:

$A = P * (1 + i)^n$ [power]. A= the amount in the account; P = the principal (which is the original amount invested); i = the interest rate; and, n is the number of years compounded.

One method to see how powerful compounding is to apply the Rule of 72. You can see how many years (or how long) you can double your money by dividing 72 by the interest rate. For example: 72 / 6% = 12 years (to double your money). 72 / 9% = 8 years to double your money. By earning a higher interest rate, you can double your money faster.

I recently read in an article where Warren Buffet provided an example of compounding: "Let me give you a figure that'll blow your mind I think. I bought my first stock when I was 11 years old. It was the first quarter of 1942, shortly after Pearl Harbor," Buffett recalls. "I spent $114.75, [for] shares [of a stock.] $114.75. If I put that

$114 into the S&P 500 at that time and reinvested the dividends, think of a figure as to what it...would be worth today?" The answer is about $400,000. So, if I as a little kid had taken that 114 bucks I'd saved— shoveling snow (LAUGH) or whatever I'd done, [I'd have] $400,000 today. [In] one person's lifetime. That's America. I mean, that isn't me. You know, it's the huge tailwind the American economy gives to any equity investor."

Also, you want to make sure to diversity your investments. You do not, as they say, want to "put all your eggs in one basket." The idea is to diversify your investments and pay as little attention to the swings in the stock market as possible. Warren Buffet said, "We continue to make more money when snoring than when active."

Diversification means to "spread around." The idea is not place all your money in one investment or stock or in one company. If you spread your investments over a number of different funds and types of investments, you will not lose it all when one goes bad. In this way, diversification lowers your overall risk.

Mutual funds and Exchange Trading Funds (ETFs) have built-in diversification that allows you to avoid placing all your money into one stock or one company. A mutual fund or ETF of an index of the S&P 500 holds the top 500 U.S. stocks, so you can see that you are not investing in just one company. But, instead, you are tracking the top 500 companies. There are index funds based on a broader market of stocks and also index funds of bonds, non-US stocks, and special types of stocks. There are also growth or value or dividend paying stock mutual funds and ETFs. The point is you want to diversify your investing.

As stated, mutual funds and Exchange Traded Funds (ETFs) provide an investor wide diversification, so you do not have all your money in one stock or one investment. You can also, in almost all cases, invest a small amount of money in either type investment, so that you can do this, as I have done, on a regular basis. These can be set up for you for a minimum amount of effort on your part. If you invest in the stock market or bond market, whether a mutual fund or ETF, there will still be risk, but the risk is minimized by the diversification of the mutual fund or ETF itself, and also among the funds you invest in.

You want to make sure when you invest in a mutual fund or ETF you are avoiding a commission (if possible). For mutual funds, you want to invest in "no load" funds or ones that do not carry an upfront fee. With ETFs, if you invest in Vanguard ETFs, as I do, and do that with Vanguard, there is not a commission. You also, as a reminder, want to minimize the fees these funds charge. The fees can range from less than a quarter of one percent to as high as three percent or more. Needless to say, you need these management fees and administrative expenses to be low. This is another reason I use Vanguard.

You are really interested in the return of the investment or how much it will earn. You cannot be certain that past results will guarantee future results, but investing in funds that match the stock market and/or pay dividends is what I have done, and I have had very good success. I have been, by following the information outlined in this Book, able to save well over a million dollars. I do not try to beat the stock market per say, and I focus on receiving a payment (dividends) from my investments.

You can contact Vanguard if that is who you elect to trade with by going online at vanguard.com or calling 800-662-7447. They can walk you through the entire process, as they did me, in setting up your account. It is really not hard or difficult. You just need to get started. Once set up, you can make your investment choices. It really can be done with little effort, and once you have it set up, it is set up. You just have to start investing or saving on a regular, consistent basis.

A little more background on Exchange Traded Funds or ETFs, because I use those for my investments (except in my 401 (k) or IRA where I employ mutual funds). ETFs are closed-end funds that often follow an index, and the expenses are typically lower than a mutual fund. You can purchase and sell ETFs just like you would a stock. You can, as I do, purchase ETFs through Vanguard. There are ETFs that track the total stock market, VTI (I invest in this one), and there are ETFs that track the bond market such as Vanguard's BND.

The average annual return from 1926 (the date of its inception) until 2010 of the S&P 500 stock index is 11.84 percent. Of course, there have been ups and downs. From 1991 to 2010, the S&P 500's average return was 10.66 percent. From 1986 until 2010, it was 11.28% and in 2009, it was 26.46 percent. In 2010, the return was 8%. These provide an idea of the overall stock market return but there are years when it goes down. However, you need to invest for the long term (5 years or more).

I have found, to build wealth, and to reach your at least one million dollars in savings objective, you have to invest on a regular, consist, disciplined basis in simple mutual funds and ETFs. It is a matter of investing in a slow and steady, regular method. Like the story of the tortoise and the hare, investing is not about chasing every new investment scheme or program that comes around. It is not about the get rich quick schemes. It is about, like the tortoise, a slow and steady process. My plan may sound boring to you, but I have written this short Book to tell you that it does work. I can attest to it. And, I truly believe it will also work for you. Please take my advice.

One of the misconceptions I have always had since graduating from school and starting my career is that I wanted to find the best, highest yielding stock that I could find if I were going to invest my money. And, with this thought in mind, I just was reluctant to invest at all. But, what I have learned is that investing success is *less about perfection and more about participation*. As long as you have time (in years, not days), the amount of time you are invested handily trumps how you timed your purchase (ie – when you got in to the stock market).

Studies from Charles Schwab have shown the following when investing $10,000 in the S&P 500 index: a) for 25 years (invested in 1990): investing at the best time in 1990 resulted in growth to $113,000; investing $10,000 at the worse time in 1990 resulted in growth to $100,000; staying in cash resulted in growth of $20,000; b) 17 years (1998): investing at the best time in 1998 resulted in growth to $29,000; investing at the worse time in 1998 resulted in a growth to $25,000; staying in cash in 1998 grew to $14,000; c) 15 years (invested in the year 2000): investing at the best time in 2000 resulted in growth to $30,000 and investing at the worse time in 2000 resulted in growth to $18,000; if you stayed in cash in 2000 the cash grew to nearly $13,000; d) 8 years (invested in 2008): investing in 2008 at the best time resulted in growth of the $10,000 to $29,000; investing at the worse time resulted in $16,000; with cash, it was basically a zero increase and the investment remained flat and you stayed at $10,0000; last, e) 5 years (invested in 2011): investing at the best time in 2011 resulted in a growth to $18,000; while investing at the worse time in 2011 resulted in growth to $16,500; if you stayed in cash, the growth was a mere $13 over your original $10,000 investment.

Participation is important, not perfection. Even investing at the worse time bested holding cash by a long shot. Therefore, you need to make sure you are investing some of your money out of each pay check you receive.

Saving a portion of your income into an investment each month takes discipline. If you do this, then it becomes a habit, and then it will become easier and easier to do. It will also make it easier to save even if the stock market declines (as the stock market will do from time to time). You can then focus on purchasing at lower prices in the event of a stock market decline, and when the stock market turns upward, your investments will grow. Further, if you invest in ETFs, or mutual funds, or single stocks that pay dividends, then your money will be making money.

Point: To attain your $1,000,000 or more in savings, you have to save money on a regular, consistent basis. Like a bill, invest on a weekly, every other week, or monthly basis. This must be your habit. Determine the amount of money you want to invest ahead of time and make the investment. You want to ensure you are taking advantage of compounding your money. Participation is more important than the "perfect" investment.

Chapter 8

Trading costs, management fees, taxes, sales commissions, and sales loads (the cost to purchase an investment) can all be a drag on your investments. You want to avoid or minimize these items as best you can if you want to reach your one million dollars savings goal.

To avoid, or minimize, the above fees and costs, I purchase and invest in passive, index funds (whether mutual funds or exchange traded funds) and buy individual stocks in good, dividend paying companies. I have found that this has been a better alternative than using a stock broker and/or an active managed funds which increase the costs of ownership.

When it comes to investing in index mutual funds or exchange traded funds ("ETF"), many experts recommend Vanguard funds. Vanguard's expense ratio pertaining to such funds are extremely low, and its management fees, commissions, and low turnover of the index funds keep expenses down allowing you to earn more on your investments. I use Vanguard for my index mutual fund and ETF investing, and I recommend it to you. Of course, there are other low cost/expense providers such as Fidelity and Charles Schwab. The point is to choose a provider that offers low fees and costs to handle your investments.

My experience has taught me that you do not need to be an expert to achieve satisfactory returns. You should, however, I have found, keep things simple. Investing does **not** have to be complicated. You do not need to swing for the fences; or in other words, attempt to get a huge profit or return on an investment. Remember the advice from the last Chapter, you need to participate in the stock market and the returns, with time, will come. At least that has been my personal experience and the advice from the financial experts.

If you are promised a quick profit on an investment, simply respond, "No, thank you." When you make an investment, focus on the future return of the investment. You should not worry so much about the daily valuations of the properties or investments but think or focus on what the investments will produce for you.

In the 20th century, the Dow Jones Industrial Index advanced from 66 to 11, 497, and it paid additionally a stream of dividends. The 21st century will witness further gains, almost certain to be substantial. Your goal, then, is not to pick individual stock winners or losers but to own a cross section of businesses in the aggregate. And, you do this, as mentioned earlier in this Chapter, by owning a low-cost index mutual fund or ETF. In fact, a low-cost S&P 500 index will achieve this goal.

I like to invest in Exchange Trading Funds (ETFs) and some single stocks. ETFs have been around for about 20 years. You want to buy a fund with low expenses, and you also want a fund that is a large in size. The Vanguard ETFs I invest in have these qualities. The experts say the worse time to buy an ETF is at the opening bell or first thing in the morning. So, do not buy them too early in the day. You can build a total, diversified portfolio with ETFs. The Vanguard ETFs charge very little. As to ETFs, I personally invest in: VTI, Vanguard's Total Stock Market ETF; VTV, Vanguard's Value Stock Market ETF; and dividend paying ETFs – VYM and VIG. I like dividend paying ETFs because they pay you for your investment; VYM and VIG are Vanguard's dividend paying ETF funds that pay you for your investment. Other funds recommended (among other funds) are: (i) VOO, Vanguard's S&P 500 index ETF; (ii) Vanguard Total Bond Market ETF (BND); (iii) you can go with an international stock fund – VXUS; (iv) a real estate investment trust, VNQ, Vanguard's broad real estate investment trust that tracks malls, hotels, and apartment stocks; and (v) iShares S & P 100 ETF (OEF) a fund that tracks the largest 100 companies in the S & P 500. It also charges a relatively low fee. However, you will need to make your own decisions. But as you read further you will find investing advice for you to reach a million dollars in savings.

As stated, the lower the fund's expenses are, the more likely it is produce bigger gains. Your total return **equals both** growth in value of your holdings plus any income that your investments produce. I like to invest in ETFs and stocks that generate income or dividends. In fact, since 1929, dividends have accounted for 43 percent of the total S&P 500 return. The advantage of investing in dividend paying stocks is that it allows an investor a modicum of control as their portfolio bounces over the sometimes turbulent stock market waves. Remember there is no surefire way to predict, much less control, stock market highs and lows and individual stock behaviors. ***But investing in dividend paying ETFs and/or stocks can give you a sense of predictability, thanks to the cash flows received from those shares***. Many corporations place an enormous amount of emphasis on maintaining and even increasing their dividend payout over time. There are many businesses that have paid dividends without interruption. Examples are: McDonald's, Proctor and Gamble, General Mills and AT&T. Dividends can also be an indicator of a company's financial health. As a wise money man once said, "Dividends don't lie."

Bonds are risky too. When interest rates rise, you will be forced to suffer the low yields until the bonds mature or sell the bonds at a substantial discount to face value. That is the reason, I personally, like investing in stable, companies that pay dividends. While their price will fluctuate up and down, the long term prospect is that it will go up and will also pay you an income stream of dividends.

Since you are getting paid dividends (and hopefully reinvesting those, as I do, until you retire), the stock market swings ought to be irrelevant. You can make and lose money when the market goes up or down because you will be investing on a regular basis (or "dollar cost averaging"). So, make sure you are investing in ETFs that provide an income or good, dividend paying companies. You need to insure you are ignoring short term fluctuations because predicting the stock markets' ups and downs is futile. The long-term returns from stocks are both relatively predictable and also far superior to the long-term returns from bonds.

Think about this. Active Income is what you produce from your activities. It is your wages, payment from the sales of goods, or services. The point of Active Income is that you have to actively work to produce money. The opposite of Active Income is Passive Income. Passive Income is the money that you produce from your investments. It is the interest, dividends, rental income, and distributions that you receive without actively working. That sounds nice, doesn't it? You want to get to the point where your Passive Income is greater than your Active Income. How do you that? You must get in the habit of investing a portion of your Active Income (and also Passive Income in the form of reinvesting it) into investments that produce interest, dividends, rental income, and/or distributions. Remember this point, you need to work to ensure that your Passive Income outpaces your Active Income.

Investing is like a snowball rolling down a long hill. At first the snowball, much like your investment total or balance, is quite small. However, as the snowball rolls down the hill, and the more it travels, the larger the snowball becomes. Same with your investment account. As you save, little by little, the investment balance starts to become larger and larger, and if you reinvest your interest or dividends, then your investment account, like the snowball, will grow larger and larger. This is the way you can, like me, reach the million dollars in savings level.

The best way I have found to build wealth is to save on a consistent basis. Saving a set amount every other week or month, each year will build your wealth over time. This is not easy to do; if it was easy, then most people would do it. Many people do not save, and thus, are not building wealth.

If you were to save $100 a month from age 25 to 65 (a typical person's working life) in the S&P 500 Index (Vanguard's ETF symbol for that is VOO) averaging 12% per year in return, you will have saved over $1 million. You would be a millionaire with saving just $100 a month. That is a typical digital television bill per month for most people. Can you save $100 per month? You can but it takes doing it. You can do this by writing on a sheet of paper a reminder to do this (like I do) and checking it off each time you deposit your money into your Roth IRA or non-Roth IRA investment account. Then, after it is maxed out for the year, place your investment money into a taxable account.

You need to start as soon as possible. Start today. Pull out a sheet of paper now. On the left-hand side write the numbers 1 to 12 (for months) or 1 to 26 for 2 times per month. Then, in the middle of the page put a column and write down the amount you intend to save. Do this now. If it is $100 each time, then put that number all down the middle column. If it is $1,000 or $50, then put that number all down the middle column. This is the minimum amount you will save consistently throughout the year. Then, in the column to the right write down what you intend to invest in. I leave this column blank and write it down as I invest the money. But placing it in an ETF based on an index, such as VOO or a Target Retirement Plan mutual fund is fine. So, your savings sheet should look like this:

Number	Amount	Investment
1	$100 (Or $50 or $1,000)	VOO or VIG or 2030 Target retirement fund
2	$100 (Or $50 or $1,000)	VOO or VIG or 2030 Target retirement fund

    The point is that you need to get started now to build wealth and reach your goal of at least one million dollars saved. You need to get started where you are. If you are age 25, then get started. The good thing about starting early in life is you will not have to save as much per month. If you are age 40 or over, do not regret that you have not started on this program yet. Start today. Get your savings sheet going. Contact Vanguard (or another low-cost provider) and get your account set up. I did it and you can do it too. Once you set up your account, then start saving. You need to get going and keep it going. If I can do it, you can too. You MUST get started. You cannot run a mile without taking the first step. You need to get your account set up, the first step, and then little by little save. It is NOT too late to start.

    A steady, monthly stream of adding to your investment fund in the amount of $200 a month or $1,000 a month, or whatever amount you have decided to invest per month, is the way to reach your million dollars in savings goal. The idea is to invest in a stock market index in equal dollar amounts on a regular basis. I have provided ideas of what you should consider investing in, but investing in a S&P 500 index ETF that Vanguard offers (symbol VOO) or a dividend, growth ETF fund (VIG) or a balanced mutual fund (STAR) is a good way to proceed, in my opinion. Plus, it has worked well for me. Some shares will be bought at a high price, but at other times, the shares will be bought low. Over a period of time, however, the funds should appreciate. Also, you want to ensure you are re-investing your dividends, so that your investment account compounds.

To become wealthy, and reach at least one million dollars saved, you have to save money. Saving money has to become a priority. You really need to just start. You do not need to try to save a lot of money at one time. This is hard. I could not do that. You have to, like me, save a little bit every other week (that is what I do) or every week or every month. Whatever schedule you pick, stick to it. You have to get into the habit of saving money. You are NOT taught this in school. But, I have taught this to you now (if you did not already know this). It does work. It worked for me, and it will work for you. Just make it a habit and trust in the process of saving little by little.

Point: To attain your $1,000,000 or more in savings, pick several ETFs that I mention in this Chapter and diversify your money in them. I use Vanguard. You can use a different, low cost provider but ensure you are investing in similar ETFs or mutual funds and do it on a regular basis (either every pay check or monthly). In this way, you will be purchasing investments on a "dollar cost average" basis. Maintain your discipline (like the tortoise) to build your wealth slow and steady.

Chapter 9

There are numerous books that will teach you about Certificate of Deposits, investing in the stock market or the commodity markets, real estate investing, and similar personal finance subjects. This Book was focused on how to save at least one million dollars. It was written in simple, easy points, so you can understand and follow them. Does it work, you may ask? Yes. It has worked for me, and if I did not think it would work for you, I would not have written this short Book. If you follow this plan, as I have done (and continue to do), I truly believe it will work for you. You will need to decide on the specific investments to make. However, I have provided some information of what I do and what I invest in.

Going over the points again, and I highly encourage you to follow this plan, is how I saved at least one million dollars or more and you can too:

1. **Point:** Avoid Get Rich Quick Schemes. They will not work. You need to avoid, based on my personal experience, multi-level marketing plans. You should avoid playing the lottery, trying to make your fortune from Publisher's Clearinghouse Sweep Stakes, inventing and trying to sell a product, investing in an untried business venture, or trying to make a quick dollar from a lawsuit. I realize that the foregoing activities have worked for some people. But they have not worked for me and for most people. So, my advice is to avoid these get rich quick schemes.

2. **Point:** You must spend less than you make. In other words, you must live below your means. You are going to have to figure out how to spend less than you make. You might have to make more money or work two jobs. Or, you might have to cut your expenses. Start with the bigger expenses when looking to cut your expenses. Start by trying to save money on your rent or mortgage and then look to save money on your car payment. Then, look at trying to save money on your car and/or home insurance. The point is you need to increase your income, while decreasing or reducing your spending, so you can spend less than you make. If you do that, then you are able to save money and reach your goal of having at least one million dollars in savings.

3. **Point:** You must get out of debt. To get out of debt, pay off your debts as soon as possible, and quit borrowing money. Pay off your smallest debt first and make minimum payments on the other debts. When you pay off the smallest debt, then go to the next one and pay it off and continue to do this until all your debt, except your mortgage is paid off. You do not want to incur additional debt during this phase. You should also work to avoid carrying a balance on your credit cards. If you cannot do that, then you need to stop using credit cards.

4. **Point:** You must have an emergency fund. You will have an unexpected expense in your life, and you will need to use funds in the emergency fund to deal with such expenses. You do not want to have credit card debt.

Outside of your retirement investing, before you start investing in a mutual fund or ETF or good, dividend paying stocks, you must build an emergency fund of three to six months of expenses. Place this money in a savings or checking account or money market account. You are not concerned about the rate of return. You need this money to avoid getting into debt, so that when an emergency comes (and it will come), you can use this emergency fund, instead of a credit card, to pay off the liability incurred.

5. **Point:** The best way to accumulate wealth (I have found) is to contribute to a retirement plan such as a 401(k), IRA or Roth IRA. You should join your company's retirement plan and contribute to the plan automatically. Pick a target retirement fund to make it easy. Increase your contributions over the year(s) until you hit the maximum allowed by the IRS code. If you are not doing, this, you need to do this as soon as possible. Make it a top priority to join your company's 401(k) plan and do it now. Have a certain percentage taken from each paycheck and contribute to the 401 (k); you can build great wealth doing this. If your company does not have a 401(k), or even if it does, and you qualify for it based on your income, then also contribute to a Roth IRA or an IRA. By doing this, you will be able to save over a million dollars.

6. **Point:** A great way to accumulate wealth is to purchase a house or condo. Do this after you have paid off debt, created an emergency fund, and joined your company's 401(k) plan. Take out a fixed rate, conventional mortgage to purchase the home or condo. Limit the loan

to no greater than 20% of your gross income and try to take out a 15 year mortgage, instead of a 30 year mortgage.

7. **Point:** To attain your $1,000,000 or more in savings, you have to save money on a regular, consistent basis. Like a bill, invest on a weekly, every other week, or monthly basis. This must be your habit. Determine the amount of money you want to invest ahead of time and make the investment. You want to ensure you are taking advantage of compounding your money. Participation is more important than the "perfect" investment. This step is where I really started succeeding and building wealth. I wish I would have learned and practiced this a long time ago. But I am a testament to the idea that it is never too late to start doing this step. You should start saving like this as soon as you can. Even if it is a small amount of money per month. The sooner you start, the sooner you get in the habit of saving and having your investments compound. Remember time is your alley.

8. **Point:** To attain your $1,000,000 or more in savings, pick several ETFs that I have mentioned in this Book, and diversify your money in them. I use Vanguard. You can use a different, low cost provider but ensure you are investing in similar ETFs or mutual funds and do it on a regular basis (either every pay check or monthly). In this way, you will be purchasing investments on a "dollar cost average" basis. Maintain your discipline (like the tortoise) to build your wealth slow and steady. This process really does work. I am not just writing this Book to provide

theories and advice to you. I have actually followed this advice, and continue to follow it, and I truly believe if you follow it too, you will attain at least one million dollars in savings.

In conclusion, you need to decide whether you will follow my advice or not. You have read my Book. I have laid out for you how I have saved over a million dollars. I have given you information that quite frankly I wish I would have learned and practiced right after I got out of school. But I did not. Now, you have that opportunity. I am a testament to the fact that this advice works and will work for you, in my opinion, if you follow it. The question is – will you heed my advice?

It is now up to you.

www.ingramcontent.com/pod-product-compliance
Lightning Source LLC
Chambersburg PA
CBHW030500220526
45464CB00006B/2598